Cara Cookie Volunteers

A Book About The Joy of Helping Others

Written by Tamara Forge ~ Illustrated by Tim Carroll

Dear Parents, Teachers and Readers,

This book was a labor of love. It is based on a true story, when our daughter and sister Cara Becker asked a really profound question at a beautiful Thanksgiving dinner. She was nine years old. What happened the next day changed our family forever and brought to her and us the absolute joy of giving and helping others in need. Service to others became a family tradition.

At age 21, Cara was diagnosed with leukemia. Even while dealing with the challenges of her own treatment, she wrote:

"All of these experiences have made me a stronger person. I've learned so much about life, about true happiness, and the fight to live. I'm confident in who I am, and plan to start my own foundation to give back and help other leukemia patients. I have big plans for the world."

And so, inspired by Cara's interest in helping others, even when she herself was in need of help, we started the Karma for Cara Foundation.

The purpose of this little book is to inspire conversation between children and their parents and teachers about how they can get involved in making the world a better place. We hope that this book can be a starting point in creating the next generation of lifelong volunteers.

The book is dedicated to everyone who is making a difference in this world by helping others, and to Cara.

May you experience the fullness of heart and love that comes from service to others,

Jill, Eric, Greg, and Jake Becker
July 2014

I know a girl named Cara with long locks of bright brown hair,
Her eyes like chocolate buttons and her nature sweet and fair.

She lives with Mom and Dad, her two doggies and her brothers –
Chewy, Happy, Greg, and Jake. They all love helping others!

She's lively like a lightning bolt,
    full of love and laughter.
She's happiest of all when she
    has someone to look after.

Today it is Thanksgiving,
    there's not an empty seat,
Relatives are catching up –
    and gearing up to eat!

Aunties, uncles, cousins fill the whole wide house with love.
Little ones play on the floor, adults chatting from above.

And what a spread there is! Turkey, stuffing, carrot cake,
But the best food on the table are the cookies Cara baked!

C ara feels so lucky,
but she can't help looking sad.
She says, "Some people don't have this,
it makes me feel so bad."

So throughout their festivities
they hatch a far-flung plan,
For helping those less fortunate
in any way they can.

But in the end the best idea
    is struck by Cara's dad,
He says, "Let's take some old folks
    all the fun that we have had."

"We'll fill the car up to the top
    with yummy food and cake,
We'll bring our groovy music
    and see what moves they make!"

Music! Food! Let's bring the residents cheer.
But beneath her smiling face, Cara faintly feels some fear.

Cara's seen the retirement home, it looms upon a hill.
Its windows great and ancient, when she glanced she felt a chill.

It's just the fear of the unknown,
    an unfamiliar place.
What if all the people see
    that fear upon her face?

She doesn't know the residents,
    will she get tongue tied?
Will they want the fun
    that Cara's hoping to provide?

Suddenly the cluttered thoughts that race around her brain,
Are shattered by an idea as it speeds by like a train.

"Instead of all this worrying for fear of the unknown,
 I'll make a list of all the things for taking to the home."

Mom has to know all the things we need to bring,
As Cara starts to write her list, she begins to sing.

We'll take...

Turkey legs and buttered rolls,
Green beans, gravy, casseroles,
Veggie treats, meaty treats,
Cheese and crackers, nuts and sweets.

Paper cups and paper plates,
Pecan pie and juicy dates,
Cookies and pumpkin pie,
Apple strudel – my oh my!

Fruity juice and fizzy drinks,
Say cheers and make our glasses clink.
Dancing tunes and microphones,
Booming amps to shake our bones!

And then as if by magic, all the frantic scribbling ceases.
Cara can relax now, that she's listed all these pieces.

The dogs are full of turkey meat and sleeping in their beds.
Her brothers have Thanksgiving flicks to fill their tired heads.

It's late now and it's bedtime, soon Cara's sound asleep.
Her list jumps fences in her head, no need for counting sheep.

No sooner has she shut her eyes than the morning sun appears,
And Cara is reminded of her current frets and fears.

But on her bedside table, neatly sitting with her pen,
Is Cara's list of items! Now she's singing once again.

"Come on down for breakfast!" Cara's mom shouts from downstairs.
"Everybody's eating, and the dogs have finished theirs!"

She digs into her favorite –
   hot waffles, fruit and jelly.
An active day is best not
   started on an empty belly.

The family is busy making
   food and packing fun.
Cara bakes some cookies,
   they're the best she's ever done.

Mom and Dad and Cara, her two doggies and her brothers,
All squash into the car, there isn't room for any others.

They bump along the road until they reach the looming hill,
But it's green and bright with flowers and a sign that reads "Restville."

The home is not so scary,
    now that Cara looks again,
And the building can't be ancient,
    it says built in 2010!

As the double doors fly open,
    Cara's flooded with good feeling.
The atmosphere is warm
    from the floor up to the ceiling!

A sweet old lady greets them, her apron reads 'Thanksgiving!'
Her walker's strewn with stickers saying, 'Life is here for living.'

"Hello there, my dears! We're all so glad you came…
It's very lovely here, but it can be a little tame."

"Let's get this party started,
    eat and eat with no regrets.
I hear you've got the doggies…
    call them in, we all love pets!"

They push together tables,
    start to get out all the food.
Play a little music, just to set
    the party mood.

Cara's brothers Jake and Greg pass around the drinks and sweets,
And the dogs are waiting patiently for petting time with treats.

"Now who's ready for a sing-along!?" Cara's mom seems quite excited.
"Pass around the microphones! Everyone's invited!"

Cara sings her favorite number, *When You Wish Upon A Star*.
Her sweet voice joined by melodies from a resident's guitar!

Cara's brothers sing together, a most wonderful duet.
Then the family is united in a rousing grand quintet.

The dogs have howled along and the staff has all sung too,
The thought of going home is making Cara feel quite blue.

But then she looks around and sees a sea of smiling faces,
It's this warm and fuzzy feeling that a true helper embraces.

She smiles at her mom and dad, her doggies and her brothers,
Cara sees they're just like her, they all love helping others.

So with a little sigh, we hear sweet Cara start to sing,
Can't you guess – she'll make another list to clean up all our things.

We'll need...

Trash bags, a litter bin –
    for putting all the garbage in,
Stack the paper cups and plates,
    put them in the recycling crates.

Microphones in their cases,
    equipment in its places.
Pack it all, stack it all,
    Don't leave any traces.

The time has come along for them to say all their goodbyes,
Cara has an odd sensation, like a stinging in her eyes.

But this welling up of liquid isn't tears from being sad,
It's the happiness of bringing people fun they hadn't had.

It's these days so full of memories that give a tale to tell,
And this won't be the last time Cara waves Restville farewell.

This great day sparked such passion that now Cara had a vision.
She endeavored to continue on her selfless helping mission.

She made a pledge to volunteer at every chance she got.
It would make you happy too, if you just tried it – so why not?

Karma for Cara

Karma for Cara is a nonprofit founded by 21-year-old Cara Becker and her family
while she was undergoing treatment for leukemia
at Johns Hopkins Kimmel Cancer Center in October of 2012.

Cara had been involved in community service since a young age, and she and her
family saw a tremendous need to help support other patients and their families
who were also challenged by cancer.

"Cara Cookie Volunteers" tells the story of Cara's first time volunteering,
based on a real experience she shared with her family.

Cara lost her battle to leukemia in December 2012.
Yet her dream for Karma for Cara lives on through the vision and works of the
foundation, her family and friends, who are inspired by her example of service and
interest in helping others even when she herself was in need of help.

All proceeds from books sold go to the Karma for Cara Foundation.
To receive a book free of charge for your school or library, email
info@karmaforcara.org.

Volunteering

Now that you know how great volunteering can be, it's your turn to get involved!

Whether it's helping out at your local library,

writing a thank you letter to a soldier, delivering a teddy bear to a sick child,

organizing a park clean up or collecting canned goods for a food bank,

there are lots of ways you can make a difference.

Try it out, and let us know how it goes!

When you tell us about how you volunteered, we'll send you a Certificate of

Membership in the Karma for Cara Heroes Club.

We'll post your name and how you gave back on the Heroes section of our website.

If you'd like to include a photo, we'll post that, too!

To tell us about your volunteer experience, email info@karmaforcara.org.

For more ideas, visit our website at www.karmaforcara.org,

and click "Get Involved."

Cara Cookie Volunteers Questions

1

What does volunteering mean to you?

2

What ideas do you have to volunteer in your neighborhood?

3

Have you volunteered before? What did you do? Did you have fun?

4

How can you inspire your friends and family to volunteer with you?

5

Why do you think Cara would be nervous to go to the retirement home?

6

What would you bring on your volunteer trip to the retirement home?

7

How many cookies did you find in the book?

Made in the USA
Charleston, SC
09 March 2016